I0473853

INFORMATION TECHNOLOGY LOGICAL ANALYSIS

ISBN: 978-1-4717-1688-1

Copyright   © Andreas Sofroniou`   2012

Copyright   © Andreas Sofroniou`   2012

INFORMATION TECHNOLOGY LOGICAL ANALYSIS

ISBN: 978-1-4717-1688-1

CONTENTS: PAGE:

INFORMATION SYSTEMS

There can be little doubt that Information System, the Internet, and Information Technology in general, is, and will be increasingly important in the years ahead.

This book has been designed for the business person, for the student and the systems professional who needs an overview regarding the logical analysis in Information Technology and the systems involved. The book explores the fundamental aspects of operational computing, the development of new information systems, and the structured methodologies used. Systems Analysis is discussed according to their structure and the book focuses on further developments in information technology and their planning.

In writing the book, the author is mostly concerned with the logical analysis and the managing of systems and people in multi-national corporations, software houses, government departments, the European Union, and academia.

In the past, the majority of data processing has been carried out by companies using batch style computer systems. With the cost of hardware rapidly reducing and with the hardware power and facilities increasing inversely, on-line and Internet systems are now becoming easier to justify and develop.

The objective of I.T. systems is to capture data, process it, and present the information. Because of the widespread use of the Internet, and all the versions of computers within business, it is sometimes assumed that data always refers to some type of financially oriented transaction. In fact, data has a more general meaning. In general terms, data can be used to denote any or all facts, numbers, letters, and symbols that refer to, or describe an object, idea, condition, or any other function. But data can only be of value if it can be organised in some way, so that it becomes meaningful to somebody; this is information.

The data must be checked for integrity, to ensure that errors have not arisen during any data capture processes. Data are compared to establish relationships, similarities, and differences. By now the data should have been completely processed, but to be proper information the processing results must be presented in such a way that it has relevance and meaning. Finally, the information must be produced on a medium that is legible.

In years bygone, on-line systems of any form have been difficult to justify because of the cost of:

- Additional hardware needed to sustain speedy response times,

- Systems software needed to support individual terminal activity,

- Additional design overhead for systems assurance.

With hardware power increasing and their costs reducing rapidly, these objectives are now disappearing.

Indeed, the justification for modern applications must be much easier now, when their benefits include:

- Speedier data entry,

- Reduced data error rates,

- Faster processing cycles,

- Quick response to user enquiries.

SYSTEMS PROBLEMS

Of all the major problems encountered in computing, the most difficult is the management of the systems and their development. Unlike any engineering or architectural drawings, the systems cannot be visibly represented as a model. Any building or machine can be shown as a set of drawings and as a three dimensional model, but the design and the build of the system cannot be seen, nor can it be represented on top of a desk.

In the case of an architectural concept, the designer will draw the plans and will supervise and delegate the tasks to builders to construct in a fashion, as close to perfect logistics as possible.

In modern computing, structured methodologies are used, where dataflow diagrams can be drawn, data can be modelled, and at the end of the logical phase, the system can be prototyped and programmed.

This brings forward the problem of managing, delegating, and guiding those who analyse the business requirements and the data on which the information is based; the professionals who proceed with the design based on the requirements and those who program and implement the required system.

In most cases, these activities are under one roof. Mainly, three different professions passing details to each other at the end of each developmental stage: Analysis, Designing, and Programming. The Information Technology Manager will need to know what each step of development involves and at every phase what the professional system engineer is doing. As in every other project, tasks need to be based on timescales and the financial implication to remain close to the budgets.

In commercial computing the financial costs for developing a new system are in six figures and in many cases where additional hardware and software are to be acquired, one project can be in the region of millions of pounds. To cope with such enormities of resources and the correct availability of business information, an organisation relies completely on the professional knowledge of its system analysts and those who manage the projects.

The media frequently report failures of systems and frustrations in computers at large. More often within companies, disappointments in systems are such that the computer department is totally isolated from other business activities. Yet, there are those companies whose total running of their business is based on the smooth running of their computer systems; the profitability and the revenue always ahead of their competitors.

But, it is also true to say that with all modern computing and devices, industry still suffers, or outputs could be improved, if only the computer department could design and operate a system the way the users work and based on the company's requirements.

The systems person is aware of these problems and yet cannot stretch his/her know-how any more than is already done. Imagine the various professionals under one roof, the complexity of designing and constructing systems, of the housekeeping involved, of the running and maintenance of all these sections.

If an organisation has many departments to enable it to function, so does the computer environment. In a superimposed mode, the Information Technology Manager has just as many sections to look after, admittedly on a smaller scale, but just as complex. Humans, machines, finances, stresses, productions, outputs, man-machine relationships, all in one department, just as much as any overall organisation is facing.

The I.T. Manager relies on management skills, systems knowledge, and various other business methods in order to give a good service to everybody in the company. The subject covers business computing and its management, the development of new systems, the implementation, and their running. The Manager in computing is aware of actual examples and will draw on projects and experience gained in building large and moderate systems based on what the users require, their problems, the solutions and their training in ensuring the success of the new system, or additional information technology modules.

In the first place, the expertise of those involved must cover the last generation of computing (which systems are still operating in many international organisations), its successes and its failures and the running in company environments. This includes the mainframe-based systems, the advent of PCs (Personal Computers) and their impact on networking and distributed processing, expert systems, shells, and artificial intelligence.

These, inevitably will be supported by training and experience in Structured Methodologies, a comparative study into methods, the use of the predominant systems architectures and a method for 'Rapid Building' system engineering.

Modern systems analysis, concentrates on the training aspect, the psychology of users, motivation and delegating specific to the computer departments, the interviewing techniques in gathering the information on current systems, the cataloguing of the problems and requirements, the appropriate solutions and their incorporation into the design of the required system.

Regarding the newcomers to the commercial computing professions, organisations rely on aspiring young graduates. With all good will they bring with them and with all their ambitions for the yuppie incomes, graduates still need the specialised training in computing and systems applications to business requirements.

It must be said that academia has progressed enormously in computing during the last ten years, but business needs differ from that of university research and studies. Graduates who enter the companies' surroundings find that they are unprepared for the demand of creating and using commercial systems in large organisations.

COMPUTING BACKGROUND

The early electronic computers of the 1940s had central processing units built up of banks of vacuum tubes, 'the glass bottles', also found in old wireless sets and television receivers. The CPUs (Central Processing Units), needed thousands of these tubes. The systems were cumbersome and unreliable, only hours between failures. There were heavy electrical power demands and the cooling plant was often as large as the computer.

The first computer of this type was ENIAC (Electronic Numerical Integrator and Computer), developed in the USA by J P Eckert and JW Mauchmy. ENIAC completed by 1946 was designed with the purpose of generating artillery firing tables. Built up of 18,000 vacuum tubes; it was immense, requiring a room 60 feet by 25 feet to hold it and weighing more than 30 tons.

In 1948, a transistor was first demonstrated by William Shockley, John Bardeen, and Walter Brattain, working in the Bell Telephone Laboratory, in the USA. Transistors could do virtually all the jobs of the then conventional vacuum tube valves, but required much less electrical power, generated very little heat and were much smaller. They were considerably more reliable and made possible the development of computers as effective functional devices in an increasingly wide range of applications.

The computers of the fifties and early sixties, individually used thousands of transistors. The various electronic components, transistors, resistors, capacitors, and diodes were mounted on printed circuit cards or boards. Copper was selectively edged from phenolic or fibreglass base to leave electrical connections between holes in which the wires of the components were inserted. A typical five-inch square printed circuit card would contain about a dozen transistors and a hundred or so other components.

Each computer (now second generation) comprised several thousand printed circuit cards. The cards, regarded as modules, were slotted into frames and interconnected by means of back-wiring. A typical large computer would be built up from several dozen specific modules, each of them being used up to several times in each computer.

In the sixties, the semi-conductor makers created a whole new technology, making possible the development of third generation computers. Using a more sophisticated version of transistor fabrication technology, it was possible to manufacture dozens of transistors together on a single small silicon chip. In this way an electronic circuit previously comprising many separate inter-connected components, could be manufactured as a single integrated unit.

By the early seventies, the basic components, transistors, diodes, etc. were assembled in a ten micro-millimetre thick surface layer in a silicon wafer. The components were then connected by metal layer evaporated on to the silicon. Subsequent etching produced a required inter-connection. Several of the integrated circuits could be mounted on a printed circuit card which could carry all the circuitry necessary for a central processing unit and the associated computer elements.

In recent years, integrated circuits were manufactured with a complexity of around one thousand transistors. The first micro-processor, produced by Intel Corporation in 1971, was based on a single quarter of an inch silicon chip which carried the equivalent of 2,250 transistors, all the necessary CPU circuitry for a tiny computer. By 1976, chips of this size using LSI (Large Scale Integration) could carry more than 20,000 components. Looking into the early part of the next millennium, the chip fabrication will allow larger chips to be built using smaller technology.

When a computer CPU is one integrated circuit, or a small number of circuits, the CPU is called a micro-processor. A micro-processor used with other integrated components forms a micro-computer.

With the introduction of Intel's Pentium and subsequent ranges, and other manufacturers' equivalent PC-based capacity and speed, together with the personal computers software such as the Microsoft hold users in amazement and difficulty in following the development in computing.

In general, all modern computers, Personal Computers (PCs), laptops, notebooks, i-pads, mobile telephones, etc. have similar architecture features, functional elements equivalent to those of an old and recent large mainframe. The PCs may vary in performance according to their storage capacity. However, these are encroaching on many application areas, formerly the exclusive province of the larger computers.

The cost of computer hardware is expected to fall even more with the development of new hardware and software in the next five years and it is expected that the resident operating languages and software will be given free as part of the hardware. Application software, in a packaged form and helpful in running commercial systems, will be of minimal cost.

Today, computing is affecting work and leisure alike, increasingly involved in factory and business operations, networking (social and otherwise), defence, medicine, education, and the domestic environment. They are influencing attitudes to privacy, employment and other social issues.

SYSTEMS ANALYSIS

The reader must remember that the construction of a system is as complex as a house built in a swamp. It requires careful planning and design. Just as a house must have an architect's plan, so does a system. It must have requirements, system objectives, and a blueprint; the Diagrammatic Representation of Systems

In general, it must be well noticed that every system structured is an answer to the users' problems and requirements. The solutions will be based on the studies of the current systems (manual and computerised), and the problems and requirements catalogue.

The design of the system will be based on how the users work and what suits the overall business environment. Whilst analysing the users' needs, the system analyst will proceed with the logical stages, by listening, interviewing, and having walkthroughs and reviews with users and colleagues.

Prior to proceeding into the physical stages development, the system analysts, designers and managers involved, will seek approval from the appropriate groups of people. Within the physical stages and during the construction of the system, the system builders will test and make the necessary alterations to the modules being implemented.

The users' systems acceptance will include all the necessary documentation and all the training and support required to ensure that the new system or module is successful.

The illustration of the generalised overall computing environment, (on the following page) can help in unravelling these complexities. The hierarchical diagram represents computing in large organisations. Within IT five major modules are included in a structured mode. Every module is diagrammatically represented, at different levels.

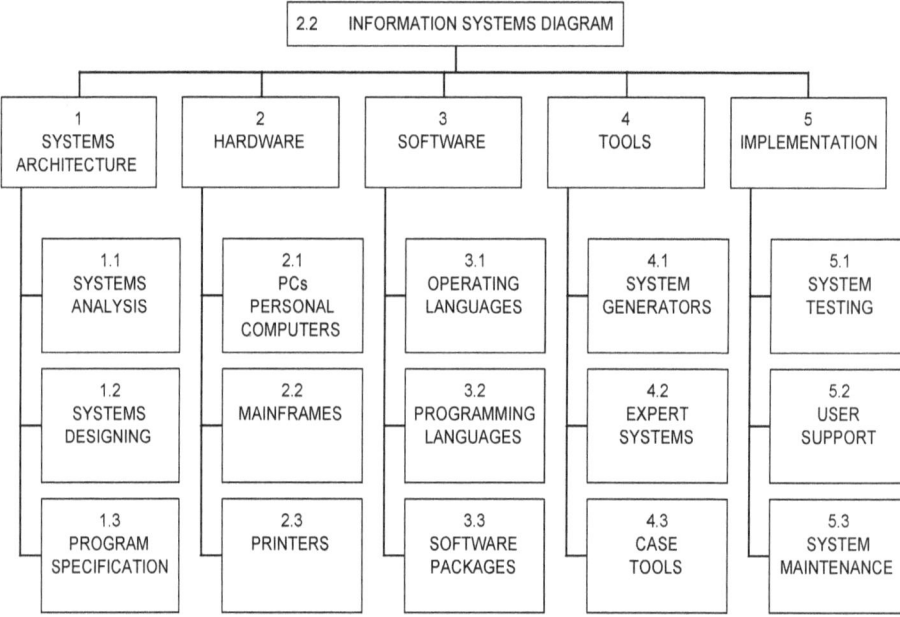

SYSTEMS ARCHITECTURE

The background of structured analysis and designing as an information engineering methodology, a technique-driven approach, started in 1972. Between 1980 and 1982, Gane and Sarson and Yourdon methodologies were extensively used. In 1983, business started using the information engineering automated version. By 1989, the information engineering development paths underwent further evolution. In 1992, the business re-engineering and object-oriented versions were introduced.

The need to control and manage the ever-increasing amounts of all organisational data being created, particularly computer-generated data, has gained recognition. However, because data management automates the processes used within a company, implementation is not easy. Several data management suppliers have begun requesting that a full systems and business analysis is undertaken prior to system implementation.

These show where existing processes need to be changed and determines exactly what the data management system needs to do within each unique organisation. It, therefore, provides the platform for successful systems architecture and management introduction and avoids the many pitfalls that so many companies have experienced in attempting to develop and install a new management system.

Rapid prototyping is gaining acceptance. Companies are using this method to obtain system design models in weeks rather than months, dramatically reducing lead-times and enabling better decisions and choice of system modules to be made.

A Systems Analyst in his/her approach defines the whole project, modularises it into manageable sections and proceeds in a logical manner according to the clear principles of user involvement.

The tasks are always broken down into structured, goal-oriented, meaningful units of work. The end result of these structured sets of tasks is applicable to the development path of:

- Information Strategy Planning,

- Business Area Analysis,

- Business Design/Technical Design,

- Construction,

- Transition,

- Production.

The above stages can be used by Analysts, Designers, Project Managers, Directors and Trainers in information technology methods to suit the technical and the user environment.

New techniques have been introduced that dramatically reduce the time taken to solve business and system problems. The result is that it is now possible to take the requirements, analyse, and view the results in days or weeks, rather than months. This, of course, makes analysis possible and cost-effective within the design process, rather than a special system task.

Recent years have seen further development in business and systems analysis software. Product releases of leading software houses have not only made systems architecture easier for everyday system engineers, but faster too. Closer links to CASE (Computer-aided Software Engineering) systems have made analysis simpler, while new interfaces make analysis understandable to users.

The term systems analysis is used in many computer installations in different ways. In fact, for most development projects it means the following:

- Fact finding,

- Operational analysis,

- Business system design.

System analysis for an organisation means that the analyst has more detailed work to do by establishing with the users that there is a justification for developing a new system.

DESIGNING SYSTEMS

The interface between the user and a computer system has always been an important design factor. In interactive computer systems the interface (the dialogue) can influence not only the system's efficiency, but also its acceptability to the user.

The significance of effective dialogue design has its advantages and disadvantages:

- Computer initiated dialogues are initially effective for the novice user, but quickly fall into disfavour when the user becomes more familiar with the system,

- Equally, touch screen icons and 'short-hand' user initiated dialogues can only be used effectively by an experienced user.

Therefore, the first aspect of interface design is to determine who will be using the system and how frequently they will be using it.

It may be necessary to have two sets of dialogues for the same system. One for the trainees, icon users, and a 'short-hand' version for experienced staff.

The user psychology here is extremely important. The interface between the user and the system must be an extension of the way the user does his/her work. Any dialogue which causes deviation from this, will cause frustration and ultimately dislike for the system.

The second aspect of dialogue design is to ensure that the system is friendly and responsive.

Friendly means that:

- Screen formats are easy to read, data entry areas are clearly identified and error conditions are highlighted,

- Computer-displayed messages on the screens give the status of user initiated functions.

Responsive means that the computer should react to a user's request within a given response time, which is normally a low number of seconds.

In summary, the design of the system is significant because:

- It affects the character of the overall systems design,

- It directly affects user acceptability,

- Once committed to a design it is expensive to change.

The new technology is introducing techniques which are changing the way organisations work, as opposed to just addressing existing tasks. To successfully implement and apply the systems tools requires extensive education and it is this that is currently presenting the biggest hurdles for companies.

SECURITY AND SYSTEM ASSURANCE

Computer security has become a challenge dominated by the improvements to information technology. Techniques are being developed to make access to systems harder. In recent years, much work has been done to make the computer recognise individual characteristics, unique to the user, such as eye contact, a signature, fingerprinting, or even the genetic print of DNA.

With users and companies becoming more dependent upon computer systems, the privacy and reliability of such systems are becoming critical aspects of design. Systems Assurance, a term which is currently popular, of a system embraces the parts of systems design which reduce the risk of both the fraudulent use of the system and lengthy recovery times in the event of a system's failure.

In many companies, one of the few problems that have to be resolved quickly is:

- Privacy,
- Fraudulent entry of data,
- Policing, a system must do more than just reporting violation,
- Effective restricted access at varying levels to different users,
- Recording access violations.

Users and companies are becoming more and more dependent upon resilience of computer-based systems. Computer systems can fail for a number of reasons.

Failures due to:

- Telecommunications,
- Hardware,
- Software,

- Networking.

Whichever the cause of the failure, the user will expect that the system can be recovered quickly and that the applications are free from data corruption.

Inconsistencies within applications can result in:

- Users losing confidence in the system,

- Lengthy investigation into the cause of failure,

- Protected systems down time whilst the data sets are reconstructed from source documentation.

Therefore, one significant aspect of recovery is the time taken to reconstruct application data sets. The most straightforward method of recovering is to duplicate them by backup. The advantage of a backup is that recovery after failure is extremely fast.

In various sensitive applications, frequent auditing is recommended. As a minimum, a daily control report should be produced, reconciling balances on the opening and closing versions of data sets. This report should also show in detail the origins of all transactions processed during the reporting period.

With the number of computer applications continuing to grow and with a similar increase in the number of people using them, a new type of back-up service is needed. To meet the demand, a number of companies have introduced guides to their applications, which include various types of catalogues. The catalogue, in fact, serves as a comprehensive system engineering tool.

Details on system applications, specifications, and service requirements are made available to all users. If a user is not sure what documents are needed, he/she can start by looking at the full index.

Companies are even making available dedicated internal e-mail messages and Internet pages, the latter being interactive and intelligent. Newsletters are published, which keep the users informed of new product developments, interesting applications, and other IT activities.

The widespread use of computers throughout business and the rapid growth of Internet connectivity mean that computer security should concern all organisations.

One simple measure to prevent unauthorised outsiders dialling into the system is to install dial-back modems. However, this security measure is easy to side-step. Likewise, calling-line identification, which permits the computer to identify the calling number and refuse access if it is not recognised, can be bypassed by the experienced people.

Encryption is essential for the transmission of any material passing down the line, broadband, and wi-fi. A simple method is to employ software which uses the same code at either end to encode and decode data. The next level is to impose a code of the day, using an encryption device card which is synchronised with a similar calculator card within the network.

The most complex form of encryption available is the digital signature. Each user has a private key linked to a public key made available on an electronic notice board. The user encodes the message with the private key and the message can be decoded by anyone holding the allocated public key. However, any message encoded with the public key can be decoded only by the holder of the private key.

SOFTWARE CONSIDERATIONS

Developing large systems require a range of software to achieve the overall objective. Depending upon the application and hardware types, this range of software at best could be totally packaged, or at worst may need to be completely written specially for the system.

Software in a project is like a jigsaw puzzle. Each piece fulfils a role and each piece must integrate with other pieces to make the complete system.

The basic types of software used are:

- Applications software,

- Conversational software,

- Database management software,

- System development software,

- Network software,

- System support software.

Applying hardware and software knowledge to system designing and the development of systems enables System Architects to choose individual applications from a range of developers and bring these together into a single system that best meets the needs of the company and its tasks, transparently, sharing data. It also enables standard software, such as spreadsheets, word-processing, presentation packages, and databases, to be linked to engineering software.

The flexibility this gives is far better for users than the traditional closed systems environment that forms the basis of many computing software packages. However, to take advantage of this environment the system developers must totally restructure their approach to system building, a complex, and daunting task.

STRUCTURED SYSTEMS ANALYSIS

As a background to structured methodology, it is worth mentioning that it all started with IBM and the problems this giant of computing was facing with the programming problems. IBM called in psychologist Larry Constantine who, as the story goes, diagnosed that the programmers were projecting their own individual perceptions of how the specifications were written.

Larry Constantine's write-up on a structured method included ideas from his psycho-physiological studies and terms such as afferent and efferent. His suggestions worked for IBM and soon after, others followed with variations. Names such as Gane and Sarson, Yourdon, James Martin, and other gurus, who again were followed by BIS Modus, LBMS-LSDM and with CCTA-SSADM and many, many more familiar names.

The differences among the protagonists were not of any consequence. Gane and Sarson used to say that all details could be gathered within a diagram and then modularise into smaller sections within boundaries. Yourdon maintained that anything bigger than an A4 paper was too complicated. Now-a-days, everybody is recommending five boxes on an average within a boundary, maximum seven and three the minimum. Any more than seven boxes and the analyst will take into consideration the possibility of decomposing to a lower level.

The point is that, instead of just picking up the keyboard of the dummy terminal and starting to program, everybody in the commercial world is now following a structured method. Whether the systems designed are successful or not, depends on the training and experience the systems engineers bear with them. In a similar way this is what the contents of this book are trying to assimilate.

NEED FOR STRUCTURED ANALYSIS

Systems Analysis consists of an evolving set of tools and techniques which have grown out of the success of structured designing. The underlying concept is the building of a logical model, a non-physical system, using a diagrammatic representation which enables the users and analysts to get a clear and common understanding of the required system. How its parts fit together and how it answers to the users' needs.

Since Computer-aided Software Engineering (CASE) tools are used to build a logical model, structured methodology involves building a system by successive refinement by:

- Producing an overall system dataflow diagram (DFD),
- Developing detailed dataflows,
- Defining the detail of data structure and process logic,

The whole of the analysis and designing of the system is done by employing a top-down method for:

- Analysing,
- Designing,
- Developing,
- Testing.

It is recognised that good development involves iteration, and an Analyst has to be prepared to refine the logical model and the physical design in the light of information resulting from the use of an early version of that model, or design. This may involve some reverse engineering of the processes of an earlier physical system, or an earlier version of the analysis exercise.

In many ways, systems analysis and designing is the toughest part of the development of an information technology system.

The problems encountered by an Analyst in a company environment will include:

- Technical difficulty of the work,
- Demand of knowledge of current technology,
- Political difficulties that arise,
- Several conflicting interest user groups,
- Communication difficulties among people of different backgrounds,
- Different views, requirements and priorities.

It is the compounding of these difficulties that makes systems analysis so demanding. It is a fact that the analyst becomes the middleman between user groups and has the intuitive approach for the users' problems and their solutions. The analyst must bring forward what is currently possible in an onrushing technology and what is optimum for the business run by people - making the match in a way which is acceptable to all.

Even with the best CASE tool, no methodology will enable the analyst to know what is in a user's mind and has no way of showing a tangible model of the system, apart from the diagrams of the logical phases and their short descriptions. On the other hand, it is hard for the users to imagine what the new system is going to do for them, until it is actually up and running, by which time it may be too late to perform any costly post-implementation repairs and additions.

To begin with, in order to ease the communication with the users, an analyst can use the tools of structured systems analysis to prepare a functional specification which:

- Is comprehended and agreed by the users,
- Sets out the logical requirements of the system without dictating a physical implementation,
- Expresses preferences and trade-offs.

The building of a logical model which clearly communicates to users what the systems will and will not do is crucially important. The users cannot afford to wait until the system is operational, before they see what they get. The analysing and designing of the logical phases are, therefore, of paramount importance in telling the users what to expect.

TOOLS FOR ANALYSIS

At a general level, it can be said that just like an existing system, the new system will represent (for example) the processing of orders from customers, the orders will be checked against a file of products available, check on a file holding a customer's details and then dispatch the goods with an invoice.

This can be shown in a logical data flow diagram (DFD):

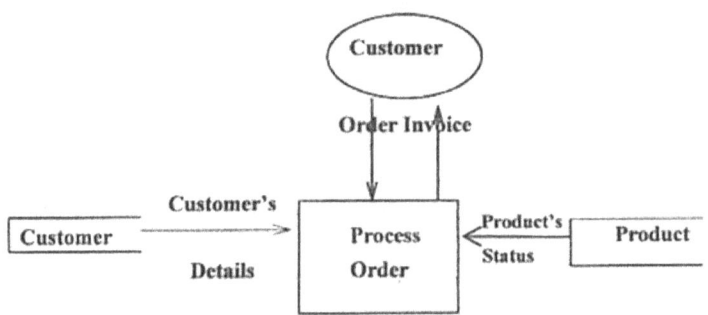

In this DFD four symbols were used:

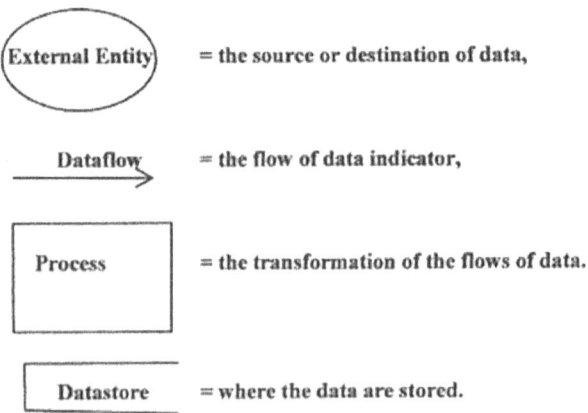

The symbols above and the concepts they represent, are at a logical level:

- An external entity may represent a client/customer, or another entity/department from within an organisation.

- A flow of data may physically be contained in a letter, or an invoice; anywhere data pass from one entity or process to another.

- A process may physically be a clerk calculating charges, or a combination of manual and automated activities.

- A datastore can be a card file, a filing cabinet, or a file on a tape or disk.

Using the four symbols enables the Analyst to draw a diagram of the system without committing the system as to how it will be implemented.

The example of 'Process Order' can be expanded to show the logical functions within the present system. The checking of incoming orders can be shown. Once the orders have been validated, a supplier can be found who is willing to give discounts on large orders.

The DFD (data flow diagram) that follows shows the checking of each order and in return the assembling of bulk orders to the supplier, to benefit from a discount. In this DFD a boundary has been introduced to separate the external entities from the activities relating to the 'handling of orders'. In a way the boundary signifies the modularisation of the processes in the functions relating to 'verifying and assembling of orders' (within the 'handling'), the data flowing to and from various 'boxes' and the storing of the data in the datastores.

The example shown is of course a summary of a lot of details regarding orders. Normally, the average of five boxes is shown within a boundary and further details are always shown in the exploded, lower level of the DFD. If necessary, each component process box can itself be broken down to a third level of detail.

Within the boundaries of the top level and the subsequent exploded second and third levels, other processes will be introduced. In elaborating the example of 'orders', processes such as 'invoicing', 'accounts receivable', 'assign shipment' etc. will be introduced.

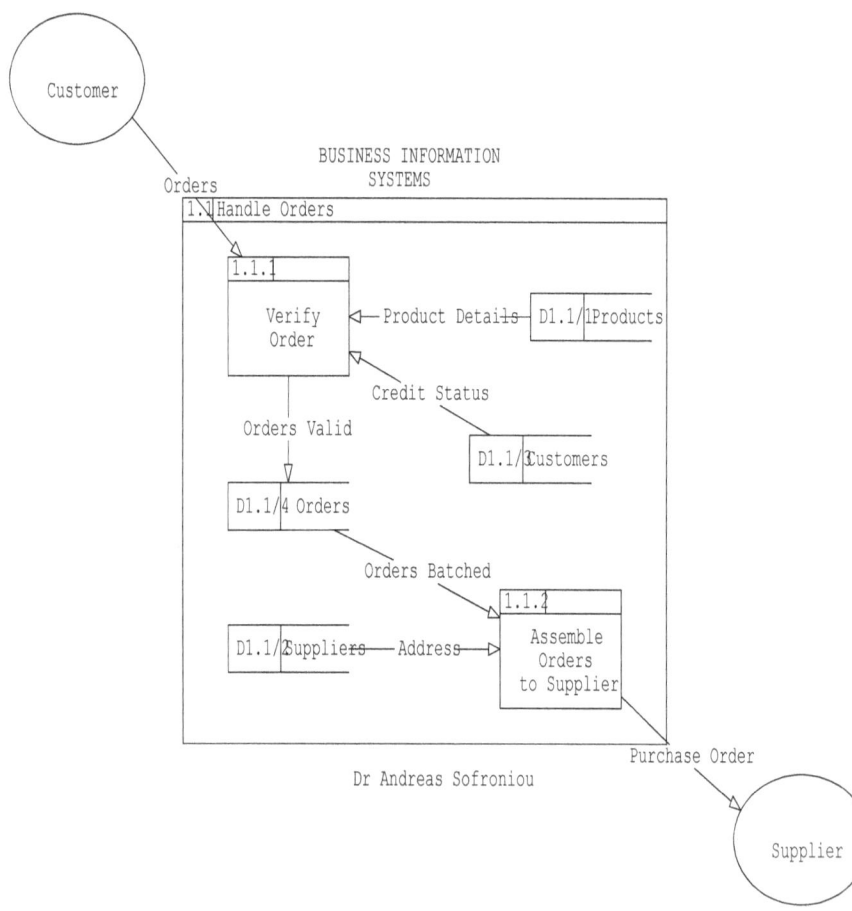

Dr Andreas Sofroniou

EXPLOSION CONVENTIONS

Each process in the top level DFD can be exploded to become a lower level DFD. Each process at the lower level will need to be related back to the higher level process, by giving the lower level process box an identification number which is a decimal of the high-level process. Thus, box number 2 is decomposed into 2.1, 2.2, 2.3, 2.4, and 2.5. Should it be necessary to go to a third level, 2.5 is decomposed into 2.5.1, 2.5.2, 2.5.3, 2.5.4, 2.5.5.

The lower level DFD is drawn within the boundary which represents the higher level process. All dataflows in and out of the higher level process must enter and leave the boundary. Datastores which are shown inside the boundary of the upper level, at the lower level DFD is shown outside the boundary.

Once the DFDs have been drawn and described, the Analyst has to decide whether a function should remain in the level shown, or identify lower level functions which are additions to the ones shown on the higher level processes.

To summarise the diagrammatic representation of an existing, or required system, identify the:

- External Entity. This involves a preliminary system boundary. Place the external entities outside the boundary, with dataflows into and out of the boundary, thus connecting the external entities with the processes inside the boundary.

- Inputs and the outputs (those arrows which represent the dataflows). What one expects in the normal course of any business. As the amount of dataflows increases invent logical groupings of inputs and outputs.

- Processes which represent the functions within the DFD boundary. The Analyst must remember that a process is triggered by a dataflow, the input of data which require a function. Once the process has undergone the transaction, the details are flowed out to be stored.

- Datastore, which can be the representative of a cupboard, a drawer, or a current system. The input of the data into a datastore can be on a temporary, or permanent basis. Whatever goes into a datastore must come out; otherwise the datastore will be the dead end of the information cycle.

USING THE METHODOLOGY

As computers get cheaper, many companies are finding that they can gain from operating systems. Additionally, many organisations find the benefit of using structured methodologies for the development of new systems. Structured analysis is useful in investigating the existing systems, be it manual or automated. The structured methods help with the understanding of the problems faced by a business and the obstacles in running a profitable environment.

Structured analysis definitely helps in deciding whether to install a computer and what parts of the systems to develop and interface the automated system with manual systems, clerical procedures other systems and perhaps suppliers' systems - customer companies' systems.

To answer such questions, maybe an initial study will assist in making a decision. Most certainly the answers will be focused on the questions of:

- What is wrong with the current situation?
- What improvements are possible?
- What are the benefits?
- Who will be affected by the new system?

In an organisation of any size, there is usually a stream of requirements from user departments for improvements in information technology services. While some of these requests can be met by improving the current systems, such as better response time, some may still bear further enhancements of the existing operating systems.

Many companies prefer to start from scratch and develop new systems and bring new ideas in running their computer systems. In such cases, the development of new systems is overdone. Many organisations find that the demand for new systems is several times greater than the resources allow.

An initial study (lasting from two days to a couple of weeks), will help to decide the route to be followed. The analyst should study the requests and meet with the managers to get the background and to begin to assess the costs and benefits of a possible new system.

It is useful to investigate the reasons for wanting to build a new system. It is fair to the analyst to remember that a new system may offer the opportunity to:

- Increase revenue,
- Avoid costs,
- Improve service.

By the end of the initial study, the analyst should be confident about the costs and the benefits resulting from a proposed system. The outcome of the initial study will be reviewed by the appropriate level of management or steering users group.

Once the go-ahead is authorised, a detailed study can begin. The detailed study builds on facts, current policies, functions, and methods of transacting a business.

The activities of the detailed study will include:

- Who the users of a new system will be,
- Functional areas considered,
- Collect views of objectives and preferences.

At this stage the building of a logical model of the current system starts and together with the refined estimates, a statement of possible increased revenue, avoidable costs, and improved services will be included in the detailed study.

As a result of this phase of the study, reviews will follow and a decision is usually made to continue the project to the next set of steps.

The definition of alternative should follow. Until the advent of structured methods, the offering of a 'menu' has not been a practical proposition, because the presentation of alternatives to users has been difficult. With structured analysis and designing, the presentation of alternative solutions involves the users in making a business decision and offers the system as an answer to what the user community requires.

The activities involved in the development of alternatives include:

- Deriving objectives from the current systems,

- Cataloguing of the new requirements,

- Developing a logical model of the new system,

Typically, the logical model by this stage consists of the overall DFD and the logical data structure. This logical model will be reviewed in detail with users and any feedback will be used to alter the documentation accordingly and will be incorporated in the design of the phase.

The analyst frequently acts as agent for the users in these phases, just like an architect will supervise the construction of a building, ensuring that the plans are being followed. The analyst will keep the logical model up-to-date, through design and implementation, especially the DFDs (data flow diagrams).

STRUCTURED ANALYSIS IN COMPANIES

There are various steps which need to be taken in order to introduce the structured techniques into a systems development organisation, with consideration to the benefits expected, together with the problems that people experienced in using systems.

The main steps involved in implementing a structured methodology in a company are:

1. Reviewing the method used for projects.

   The amount of work involved in assessing the procedures used in systems development will vary greatly, depending on whether a formal structured methodology has been adopted, or whether the organisation has created its own ground rules.

   Any method based on structured analysis will specify a sequence of activities to be followed in creating a system, the products to be developed at each stage and the management controls to be applied. Almost any established method will, in general, specify the conduct of a feasibility study. Following a feasibility study, a detailed design, followed by coding and testing.

   If such a methodology is already used, check that:

   • It does not encourage pre-mature physical design. If so ensure that this is modified to allow for the logical stages to be introduced prior to entering the physical stage.

   • The methodology in existence does not subscribe to over-documentation - the exhaustive narrative details. The DFDs and data modelling can easily replace the excessive writing and descriptions.

   • The present method allows for top-down development. This point raises a more fundamental issue. That of the 'straight-line-approach'. Many systems engineers assume that a well-managed development project goes in a 'straight line', from the feasibility study to the analysis, through design into testing and users acceptance. The path of such a project can be completed by using a 'spiral' approach.

The spiral concept reflects the reality of the problems faced in systems development. At each progressing phase a skeleton is built, this is then logicalised and walked through to see how well the logical phases work and then reverse to put more details into the study. Thus, the project control needs to accommodate the delivery of sensible products; dataflow diagrams, data structures and functional analysis, rather than the completion of activities.

2. Establish standards for the use of a CASE (Computer-aided Software Engineering) tool.

A decision may have to be made to acquire a CASE tool. This is a good support for the Analyst's responsibilities in diagramming the system-to-be. It is very convenient to have a tool for diagrammatic representations for the maintenance and easy updating of diagrams and specifications in general.

CASE tools are progressing so quickly, the latest versions include the facilities for quick prototyping and transforming the descriptions to structured English and in turn to 4GLs coding.

3. The tools and techniques of structured systems analysis must be as simple and as realistic as possible. To use any system engineering techniques expertly needs experience; study and practice. While the rules and conventions can be learnt easily, the hardest thing appears to be at the logical level.

Whatever the difficulty, a DFD showing sequence of events improves the understanding of the users, thus the analyst's tasks become much easier. In analysis and design users are asked to think about problems at a higher level of abstraction and this can take time and persistence.

Apart from the fluency with the logical tools, the analysts need to become familiar with the emerging support software. If the ground rules for projects are to change, analysts will have to explain them to the users. Analysts need to be briefed on new methodology and think through its implications for users.

If structured development is to be used, the analysts must be thoroughly briefed on the concept and the implementation plan of each project with which they are concerned. The analyst, most certainly, must be able to criticise a design in the light of the structured methodology principles.

4. As the new structured techniques and approaches improve communication with users and involve them more in setting the direction of the project, they are welcomed by the user community. At the same time, the new ideas represent a change in the rules of developing systems, in a positive way, as the implications and benefits are clearly explained in the process of designing.

The communication with the users, as each 'structured' project starts, should cover the following points:

- Notation of the DFD,

- Concept of presenting a 'menu' of alternative systems for the users to consider,

- Briefing on the structured method,

- Warning on the participation and involvement required on the part of the users,

- Reassurance that the new method for system development does not impose more effort,

- New project will not generate more paperwork for the users.

In some companies, the users are trained to draw their own DFDs and their own descriptions in structured English. The analyst ought to encourage this, provided the individual user wants to go ahead with this. This concept, in many organisations, proved very beneficial, in as much as the communication difficulties experienced prior to this method, they just disappeared. The users felt as if they were guiding the project the way it suited them.

Where specific executives are assigned as members of the Users Committee, it is desirable that they should be trained in structure methodology. This will give them the ability to present the business, their point of view, and the requirements, subsequently defining them to the analyst. The Executives trained in structured analysis can be more informed critics of the logical models produced by the system engineering area.

With structured training, the users will be able to quantify most of the benefits that result from improved productivity and the better management time and resources.

The benefits from using structured systems analysis, from the system architecture point of view, are even more profound:

- Users get a much more vivid idea of the proposed system from logical DFDs, than they do from narratives and excessive descriptions,

- Presenting the system in terms of logical DFD reduces the misunderstandings and issues,

- Interfaces between the new system and existing systems are shown clearly by the DFD and the data model,

- Use of logical models eliminates duplications.

The benefits, of course, are not free from potential problems. The problems may be partly due to the change in working procedures and partly the result of the discipline imposed by the logical phases.

This type of problem can easily be reduced by:

- Introducing training to the users and the analysts as early in the project as possible,

- The effort and degree of detail required, especially in building the data model is often resisted. The consolation here is that, if the data are right in the first attempt, then less effort will be needed in the latter stages of development,

- Where structured English are introduced, programmers feel uneasy and often complaint that all fun is taken out of programming and that they become mere coders. The uneasiness goes away when the programmers see that structured systems give them more work to do, by bringing forward their responsibilities, during the designing stage.

- Introducing structured techniques for analysis, design and development, starting at any point in a project.

RAPID BUILDING METHOD

A quick method for building systems, using structured design techniques make for better systems, at lower costs, by providing techniques for detecting and correcting errors as early and as cheaply as possible.

Although quicker, it still means going through the structured analysis, designing, top-down development, structured coding and having structured walkthroughs. What it means, is that the system analyst tries to cut down the unproductive use of professional time by matching what is possible with what is worth doing.

To manage such steps requires a lot of experience in the whole system development lifecycle and at each step the following thoughts ought to be raised:

- The system being built is of a technically excellent status, but is this what the users want?

- The users were given what they asked, but could the Analyst have done so much more for them?

In approaching the quick way of developing a system the analyst needs good probing techniques. He or she must find out the factors which stand in the way of achieving the objectives. The factors which would be impacted by better, faster, richer information.

It is a fact, that unlike other business projects, system analysis cannot produce a model. In complex construction projects, a scale model is built and everybody concerned can get a vivid idea of what the final building will look and how their interests will be served.

In information technology this can be done by diagrammatic representation, demonstration of dataflow diagrams and screen prototypes.

'Boxes' as symbols are used as the tools of structured analysis in a DFD (Dataflow Diagram) form, where they fit together as a logical model of a system, at any level of detail.

The symbols involved are:

- External Entity (outside the boundary),
- Dataflow,
- Process (Each process within the boundary can be exploded),
- Datastore.

The quick building method relies heavily on the composition of Structured English, which in turn depends on the:

- Functional decomposition,
- Lowest level - decomposed DFD,
- Entity diagram,
- Descriptions.

The details extracted from all four above will 'sieve' into Structured English.

These in turn, have their own conditions and actions:

IF condition - 1

THEN action - A

ELSE (not condition - 1)

action - B.

In nested 'Ifs', using 'AND-IF', the following example may help:

IF you need a holiday

AND-IF you can afford it

AND-IF you have somewhere to go

THEN take a holiday

ELSE (you have nowhere to go)

As a rule of thumb, in writing Structured English please do not nest more than three levels.

The role of the analyst in all this is of great importance.

A well trained, ethical individual with about five years experience will be able to:

- Help in devising the system versions and speak for the users' interests,

- Explain the top-down development concept to the user community,

- Ensure management support for timely systems development,

- Exert pressure for frequent, full integration of sub-systems,

- Ensure that the sub-system is developed top-down,

- Act as the users' representative in accepting each version.

Based on the procedures standards defined in the next chapter, the Analyst will carry out an analysis of the present systems operations and identify the problems.

This exercise will include the:

- Computer system,

- Manual system

- Combination of both.

This stage will be followed by the specification of the required system where the requirements are consolidated and the chosen option is defined in detail. In parallel to this, the required data structure is created.

SYSTEMS MANAGEMENT

The majority of organisations recognise that the effective use of information is vital to their success. Successful companies build enormous knowledge bases that reside in their corporate files, their information centres and in the brains of their busy executives. This knowledge and experience is the organisation's power base and their competitive edge.

To remain competitive they must be able to find information at the right time, in the right place and in the format that is easy to use..

The management of the information systems must ensure:

- Availability of the information,

- Services that enable this,

- Effective use of technology,

- Supply of the skills and time needed.

When the IT department manages the information derived from the systems, effectively, the company in turn gains real value from information. The IT department and its management of information must maintain a leading position in the specialised world of commercial computing.

The IT department will certainly benefit by having a network of specialists providing knowledge, experience, and technical skills to suit most types of company demands.

In managing IT professionally, the benefits will include the:

- Capturing of the knowledge already in the organisation,

- Making this knowledge accessible to those running the company,

- Developing the appropriate strategic plans and systems,

- Protection of the information supplied by the systems,

- Accuracy and recoverability of all data,

- Recruitment, training, and developing the system analysts.

Instant access to corporate information means better decisions, reduced costs, and increased profits. To facilitate such a service, the IT department must work with a wide range of other departments and their staff. Many of the users are looking for help or advice from the information management area.

This means that the IT staff must be prepared to undertake all sizes of projects, their development, and the management of such systems. This entails a project management system which, together with the chosen methodology, will ensure the success of the information services.

MANAGEMENT OF PROJECTS

A project management system should be utilised on all sizeable projects undertaken. A Project Manager should be appointed, responsible for the agreement and delivery of project products to agreed deadlines throughout the project's lifecycle.

The main project management issues include:

- Proper user, staff and management training,
- Management commitment,
- Budgets,
- User and expert time,
- Identify key users,
- Schedule time for analysis and design,
- Establish metrics,
- Small teams.
- Testing implementation and handover to users.

The Project Manager should produce a weekly status report which will be provided one day prior to a weekly progress meeting.

This report will have the following format:

- Milestones, summary report of the current and previous status of milestones,
- Progress, a narrative of progress,
- Changes to the project baseline, including change notices,
- Issues, details reported for current week and the status of those previously reported,
- Variances in either time, or effort for any milestone,

- Resource usage for the week,

- External factors that may impact upon progress, but not within the control of the project management,

- Cost reports of any costs incurred during the week, excluding resource costs and known regular costs,

- Objectives and risks for the next period,

- Recommendations and issues for discussion.

The weekly meeting should take place between the:

- Users' Project Manager, or representative,

- System Project Manager, or representative.

During the project lifecycle, project issues can occur which require analysis, documentation and resolutions. Project issues fall into those that occur during the:

- Development and delivery of the system,

- Operational life of the system.

Any change to the requirements, or to any document once it has been formally agreed, is subject to the following change control procedures:

- A change control notice will be raised by the user requesting the change,

- An estimate of the impact of the change on the schedule and costing of the project will be prepared by the system Project Manager,

- The change details will be transmitted to the users representative for authorisation,

- If the change is authorised, then the change control notice will be annotated by the member of the project team, who implements the change to indicate that it has been completed. A copy will then be filed with the documentation affected,

- The documentation itself will be updated to reflect the change, with update pages sent to all nominated parties,

- All changes during the project, whether by the user, or system developer will be controlled by the IT project area.

Throughout the life of the project, reviews of critical documents are necessary. The procedures for review of these documents are as follows:

- All critical documents will be reviewed within the project team structure to ensure adherence to the project standards,

- The quality to be randomly selected and reviewed by the Assurance Manager,

In case of controlled documents, this will include a check that the documents have the following details:

- Document identification,

- Document name,

- Name of system Project Manager,

- Distribution list,

- Current version.

The strategy of the system acceptance will be defined by the user. The subsequent plan and test scripts will be based upon the standards. As part of a quality management system, a senior manager undertakes the auditing of the project. The quality auditor operates outside the design and builds team structures.

Before delivery of the system, a training schedule for the users will be agreed. Additionally, prior to any handing over, the system will be tested and should any problems arise, these will be reported and remedied before the users sign off.

RECRUITMENT AND INTERVIEWING

With the state-of-the-art in logical analysis, the accelerated progress in technology, and the demand made on more systems development, the IT management find themselves increasingly occupied in the selection of larger number of specialised staff. Such is the great weight on IT managers, to fulfil new job responsibilities and to replace those who leave for greener pastures.

The vacancies for system analysts are constantly increasing, at such a rate that a new industry has developed. Additional to the traditional recruitment, the demand for the supply of contractors, mainly for systems analysis and programming, has increased in proportions. Agencies for freelancers are now deeply rooted as a service to IT.

The contracting analysts are in their thousands and agencies in their hundreds. The cost to the organisation for such a service is huge, often enough remuneration paid being higher than what the business directors are paid. Frequently more than the IT manager gets. With such numbers of candidates involved and an unknown expertise at that, the systems managers are faced with the additional responsibility of frequent interviews and uncertainty as to what kind of know-how they will obtain from contractors.

The agencies do not have the knowledge to scrutinise every systems analyst on their registers. It is a well known fact that the agents submit the CVs of individuals without even checking on the contractor's experience. The agencies arrange for the interviews between the company's managers and the freelancers over the telephone. For this kind of service the agencies receive between 20% and 40% of the contracting fees. The larger, established contracting agencies have a firm charge of 33% commission.

The IT management and their staff are faced with the overload of interviews. It is an under-estimated task. With all the pressures from within the systems areas, it is a wonder how systems can be developed and become operational within the quoted timescales and costs.

As an example (using the two extremes of the systems professions), the analysts, and programmers, it is of paramount importance to use the right techniques for interviewing systems staff. In hiring systems professionals, it must be remembered that an analyst is the person who keeps in touch with the users and the programmer is the one that builds the system.

The analyst must be an outgoing person, a good mixer - a person who can get on with other people, easily collect information, and must be a good systems representative. This is a psychological personality type of an extrovert thinker.

On the other extreme, bear in mind that the programmer has to decipher the documents the analyst produces, in order to start constructing the required system. This makes the programmer the psychological personality of an introvert sensation type.

There are many other types of professionals within systems development. The list includes designers, database administrators, operators, strategists, and a few more. In interviewing, therefore, the interviewer will be helped enormously if he/she makes a few notes beforehand regarding the type of person needed to fill in the responsibilities within the systems professions.

In interviewing, handing out a short narrative and asking the interviewee to turn it into diagrams and programming coding is not on. The candidate must be relaxed, made to feel wanted, important and then prompted to expand on items relevant to the vacancy.

Systems building is such a modern profession, its responsibilities and qualities are hardly known to psychologists, psychometrists, and professional recruiters. For instance, one cannot rely on aptitude testing alone, as there are no set rules. Experience in systems areas and knowing what is needed is the best guide and basis for the interview.

Within the various scales of recruitment are the newcomers to the professions of systems management: The graduates of IT 'hybrid' management and the MBAs, whose degree material is based on traditional management. I.T. logical analysis demands organisational experience gained within business functions relating to systems.

The young graduates of the first degree education can be recruited with the proviso that they get trained within the business parameters. It is true that the new universities in their computing sciences subjects cover methodologies, databases and programming, but the question still prevails; the extend of commercial experience embedded in the lecturers and their tutorials and those running the academic departments. Let it be stressed that this statement refers to the business computing and systems development in the commercial world.

Universities have progressed enormously in their research on artificial intelligence and other fields such as parallelism. The outside world still runs systems on mainframes and applications as required by the users. The modern construction of business systems and tools developed, suit the personalities and the abilities of those who use these applications.

Faced with such problems, the IT management pays a lot of attention to interviewing. After all, like any other recruitment, employing a human being (permanent or contractor) is still a big investment of time, costs, and other resources.

It must be added, that the interviewing techniques in commercial computing are applied to applicants for vacant positions, as well as the users who ask for new systems, the repairing of an existing one, or the extraction of the data based information.

Interviewing is the most commonly used way of acquiring basic concepts and requirements from the users. It is an activity that needs careful planning and execution. It is crucial to plan an interview to ensure that it is as productive as possible.

Whether interviewing an applicant for a vacancy, or a user for his/her requirements, it is worthwhile bearing the following in mind:

- Ensure that the interviewee is prepared for the interview,

- Notify the subject to be covered,

- The time and location of the interview,

- Probable length of the interview,

- Ensure that a room is ready, away from the interviewee's workplace, thus minimising distractions,

- Make the interviewee comfortable with the computing terminology and jargon,

- Build a rapport, listen, and show interest.

As an interviewer, practise the art of relaxation on you and then apply the technique to the candidate. Remember that the users' interviewees may offer details on what they think you want to know. A good analyst will steer the discussion to the domain of interest, whereas a job applicant will be nervous, anxious and feel as if on the receiving end.

PROJECT CONTROL IN DEVELOPING SYSTEMS

Businesses have problems which they need to solve. They, also, have requirements which altogether enable the smooth running of their environment. To establish the appropriate running of the business organisation, projects need to be set.

An organisation is probably undergoing significant changes. Changes span functional boundaries, case conflict, and concern and present a major risk to the business and those managers responsible for the development of systems. Many companies are now adopting a project-based approach to managing the change of systems and their development.

Managers of today and of the future, require skills in managing projects. These skills are supplementary to the line management skills. A company needs to enhance business planning and control structures to explicitly link system implementation to business led projects and programmes.

A project in information technology is a temporary situation within the working groups (the system users) and the computing management, with the objective of delivering a product. The resulting product relies on the project progress and how it is approached in its scope to deliver.

For a project to be successful it needs:

- Management at all levels,
- Team building and staff motivation,
- Planning and controls,
- Quality standards to follow,
- Communication between users and management,
- Objectives and scope,
- Adequate skills and experienced resources,
- Explicit documentation and training.

Unlike existing systems operational management, where one deals with established computer services, project management encounters the unfamiliar, new problems and needs for change.

In managing a project, a list of activities will not be enough. The project must be product-based. A methodology needs to be followed, procedures to be applied. The appropriate procedures, therefore, give the advantage of common standards being applied to the management of all projects, with directional emphasis to meeting the corporate objectives.

Always remembering that a system is built with quality and that the application of the procedures and techniques must be flexible and practical:

- For the users,

- To fulfil a process,

- Benefit the business function.

Project management supports the implementation of the business strategies with explicit link to the development plan. This provides management with the ability to react swiftly and efficiently to any changes, to understand the project stages and steps in hand and their relationship with each other. It, also, provides an effective way of controlling costs and resources at all levels.

The appropriate analysis and design methodology will assist the project team members to concentrate on the system components to be produced. It enables the management and the analysts to identify and clearly define all the development phases. It is, also, a significant contributor to quality, better estimating, and planning.

This means that a systems manager and his/her team members need to establish project control standards, which will specifically include:

1. Purpose,

2. Scope,

3. Input,

4. Planning,

5. Progress control.

1. Purpose:

The purpose of the project control standards is to define the standard to be used within system development for managing the project in terms of project planning and progress control.

The objectives of project management being:

- Establish clear objectives and scope for a project,

- Ensure roles and responsibilities are well defined and understood,

- Break work down into schedules and deliverables,

- Plan how an individual project will achieve the implementation of the required end product within a progressively refined and agreed schedule and budget.

A project control framework is necessary within which project management skills and techniques are exercised.

2. Scope:

This standard addresses Project Control in a new system development environment, i.e. a multi-team situation with Team Leaders and an overall Project Manager.

It covers the planning of each phase for each team and its members and the progressing of those plans.

3. Input:

The inputs will vary with the size and stage of development:

- Terms of Reference (ToR, for a new project) and Project Initiation Document (PID),

- Key documentation from earlier phases (for an existing project)

- Procedures manual

4. Planning:

The following steps describe a team leader's project control, carried out at the start of a project, or when rescheduling (as a result of supplying more tasks, or changing estimates).

- Task Identification. A source of information for this will be the overall project plan and the activities listed.

- Estimating. Estimating for project control planning is carried out using the bottom-up approach, starting with the steps involved and building upwards. When all tasks have been identified and estimated, an overall schedule can be drawn, which accounts for resource constraints, deadlines and overheads.

- Scheduling. The basics of scheduling are to take the information from task identification, sizing, and resource allocation and to build a schedule which meets the necessary timescales.

5. Progress Control:

The Project Control system and progress meetings are the principal mechanisms for monitoring and controlling the progress of a project.

- Progress Meetings. Aside from the informal contact maintained between a team leader and team members, each person should receive a regular progress meeting, on a one-to-one basis. Also, each team leader should meet with the project manager on a similar basis.

- Team Meetings. A regular weekly meeting of all team members is important, in order to maintain communication and to resolve issues where input is required.

- Outstanding Issues. As projects progress, design issues may emerge which require a solution. At the end of the development, any loose ends not resolved can be passed to the support team for future enhancements to the system.

- Rescheduling. Even the best planned project may have its scope changed by changes in requirements, or late design changes. Changes of this type can cause disruption which outweighs the benefits they provide, so it is important to keep them to a minimum.

SYSTEMS DEVELOPMENT PROCEDURES

The system specification procedures form the basis within the conventional business environment as these sets out the standards for system development. They describe a step by step approach to developing and implementing computer systems. They define the documents to be produced, the controls to be applied and the tasks to be performed.

The intention is that these procedures be applied flexibly. On the other hand, the phases are designed for sequential development, with the output from one phase being the input to the next, all leading to the eventual implementation of the system. Project plans should be drawn up to suit the particular project and then adhered to.

The procedures define the paths that will be followed in projects set up to develop computer systems. A project is, thus, described in terms of its major divisions (Phases), its Control Points, the Activities that are accomplished in each phase, and the tasks that go to make up those activities.

A project starts with an initiation and ends with a review and user training. The Project Initiation Document (PID) will incite the feasibility study and the terms of reference. The review will include the report to the users and the appropriate steps for the system training and the training manual distributed to all the users involved in the running of the system-to-be.

Otherwise, the project has the following phases:

- **Business Analysis:** Users' business Problems and Requirements and the initial top level Dataflow Diagram.

- **Systems Analysis:** System Proposal, Functional Decomposition, Dataflow Diagram, Logical Data Structure and Process Descriptions,

- **Design Options:** Technical Design Options,

- **Functional Analysis:** Process Model, Detailed Dataflow Diagram and Process Descriptions,

- **Data Analysis:** Data Model, Entity Life History,

- **Physical Design/Build,** System Specification, Program Code.

The system development lifecycle, in outlining the activities to be followed and the tasks to be carried out in a project, provides the framework for planning and defining a project.

The development lifecycle does not ensure that projects will meet a particular level of quality, nor does it ensure that work carried out will be both, efficient and effective. That is a matter of how people perform and it is the goal of project management to make sure that conditions exist for them to be efficient and effective.

The framework of the lifecycle with its different phases, offers some guidance on when project management should be applied. Each phase has a beginning, middle, and end. Project management procedures are ongoing and required to fit in with the dimensions of the workday and reporting cycles.

Project management is a series of activities that are carried out during a project by the leader:

- Planning,
- Estimating,
- Monitoring,
- Reporting,
- Quality control,
- Resource allocation,
- Communication.

The performance of any computer department can only be judged by the service given to the system users. This means a variety of business changes through projects. It involves people and the experience they carry with them. Experience in system building when a company needs it most; when this type of people, the best in the organisation is in short supply and great demand. They are usually, therefore, not available when needed for a critical new project - to develop the long awaited system.

SYSTEMS SPECIFICATION

The System Specification starts as systems analysis and is not completed until programming begins. A standard is required for conducting systems design because a uniform approach is needed across all projects to ensure understanding and consistency.

The standard outputs are required as input to programming activities. The systems specifications, therefore, need to be written in a rigorous and consistent manner to ensure that all user requirements are catered for and all business processing is completely and accurately defined and documented.

The following may be input to system specification:

- Current, systems documentation and specifications,

- Users' requirements documentation and proposals,

- System proposal from system analysis phase,

- Process descriptions, dataflow diagrams and layouts from the functional analysis phase,

- Minutes of meetings with users.

The System Specification is the phase where the lowest level dataflow diagrams and descriptions from process analysis are pulled together.

PROCESS ANALYSIS

The aim is to reach a detailed logical design sufficient for all specification work. A standard is required for conducting process analysis because a uniform approach is needed across all projects. It concentrates on processes rather than data. Thorough process analysis encourages understanding of the system and user environment. The outputs from the process analysis are required for the system design processes.

There can be many inputs into process analysis depending on the nature and complexity of the project. The following may be input to process analysis:

- Systems documentation and specifications from the current system,

- Users' requirements and proposals

- Decomposition of dataflow diagrams.

The dataflow diagram is a powerful input to design because it identifies the data flows, data stores and processing involved. The technique is top-down; an overview followed by increasingly lower levels of detail.

SYSTEM REVIEWS

The purpose of a review is to define the process for understanding what is required: Also as a method for checking the quality of work throughout the systems development lifecycle.

The objectives of holding a review of a piece of work are to:

• Ensure the work meets its requirements,

• Trap errors as early as possible,

• Provide a focus on outstanding issues which lie in the pathway to completion of a given task,

• Check adherence to standards.

It is clear that in practice it would not be appropriate to subject all outputs to the same level of review and several variants of the review process are required.

The different levels of review allow for the:

• Importance of the review material,

• Authority of the attendees,

• Level at which the review is documented,

• Formality with which the review is held.

PHYSICAL DESIGN

Physical design converts the results of process and data design into a computer solution for implementation and defines the computer/clerical interface. This is evaluated against the requirements and amended as appropriate.

The scope of the physical design is to cover the technical design of application systems. It concentrates on the design of the system processes, rather than the design of databases.

The following may be input to systems design:

- Current systems documentation and specifications,

- Users' requirements and solutions,

- System proposal from analysis phase,

- Process descriptions, dataflow diagrams and layouts from functional analysis phase.

Requirements often change during the design phase and new ones emerge. In addition, it often raises more questions requiring further analysis. Therefore, the final design may only be arrived at through several iterations of logical and physical design.

QUICK DATAFLOW DIAGRAMMING

Dataflow diagrams (Dfds) are used for process analysis, to show the logical:

- System processes, hierarchy and their relationships,

- Datastores, the system's data 'at rest',

- Data flows, the system's data 'in motion' between two processes, or between a process and a datastore.

To present a complete system description, additional documentation is necessary for each flow, each datastore, and each process.

It is the DFD which structures the analysis process and drawing the DFD helps the analyst to:

- Deal with the information collected during data gathering, in an orderly manner,

- Avoid being overwhelmed by detail and losing sight of the overall picture,

- Document the proposed system in a convenient format as input to design,

- Communicate with users.

PROGRAM DESIGN

Before they are coded, programs need to be designed. There needs to be a structure which shows how and where the processes diagrammed in the DFD and described in the System Specification are to be performed.

Structured English is used to represent the design. This is a simplified form of English, presented in defined manner. Within the structure so formed, normal English is used, although in as succinct a form as possible.

The relevant systems specification proceeds to a program design ready for coding.

To enable this, the following inputs are necessary:

• Decomposition diagram,

• DFDs at the program or transaction level,

• System specification,

• System flowchart,

• Data structure diagram.

A program design which is structured is easier to maintain and understand. The structuring of the design means principally that the design should be driven by the flows of input and output data.

The program designer or programmer should arrange for regular program and code Walkthroughs with another programmer/designer.

The walkthrough session should check:

• Adherence to programming standards,

• That the code matches the design structure,

• The code performs the processing defined in the system specification,

• Database accessing is correct.

Program designing and programming in general, requires disciplined management since this needs clearly defined objectives to fulfil the overall project.

Project management must, therefore, ensure that the investment of resources, time, and effort are fully justified and fulfilled. This includes program definition and the setting up of efficient structures. Whatever the requirements, experience is of major importance in helping and controlling programming

OVERALL OBJECTIVES

As organisations strive to increase productivity, to reduce costs, to shorten cycle times, to improve product and service quality, so the demands made on systems for modifications and for new information increase. Being able to make better decisions based on quality information and having the flexibility to respond to new opportunities increasingly, depends on having the right systems in place at the right time.

Applications developed based on older technologies may well not meet current requirements in some or many areas, such as:

- Functionality,
- Ease of use,
- Data access,
- Maintainability,
- Flexibility,
- Robustness,
- Costs.

With the wide range of application environments and building blocks now available, it is still possible to have an affordable system designed and built to meet specific business requirements. This gives the flexibility and control to define the system the way the users want it and then to change and adapt the system to support the business over coming years.

Computer-aided Software Engineering (CASE) tools address the application design stage. For business systems they can be extremely useful to assist in the design of both, the application and the data structure.

Rapid Application Development (RAD) techniques incorporate a series of steps which business people and Information Technology professionals work through together to develop a prototype of the application representing the business process before full scale development.

The objectives of analysis is to understand what a particular area of the business does and how information is exchanged, created and modified by business processes.

With a clear understanding of the information needs of a business area, the system engineer can determine which business activities to automate and then develop those systems so they meet end user requirements.

The design helps users move from a logical representation of 'what' a given system is to perform, into the physical specifications for 'how' the system will actually be implemented.

In order to handle the complex nature of a system, it is often helpful to break down the processes and data of the system into manageable pieces. Decomposition diagrams are an easy way to partition the data and process requirements of the system, by analysing and application, refining high level business processes into lower level processes. These processes can then be broken down further until the analyst reaches a level of detail where a process can best be described in terms of its procedural logic.

The analysis stage is unique in its approach to integrating the process model with the data model. The analyst can build the application data model by defining, one at a time, the data model for each individual process.

Dataflow diagrams can help describe how a business area or system functions. They show how data flows into and out of the business area or system, how processes transform data and the external agents (recipients/sources) that interface with the system.

Entities are the subjects of information (people, places, things) about which a business needs to keep data. An entity diagram provides a graphic way of describing the data requirements of a system and how they interrelate. The entity diagram, also, helps describe and characterise the relationships among these entities.

COMPUTER-AIDED SOFTWARE ENGINEER (CASE)

In many Information Technology (IT) departments, the complexity of applications often dictates that development responsibilities be divided among members of a project team. The ability to share information is a fundamental requirement for systems development tools.

Such tools, Computer-aided Software Engineer (CASE - some system engineers describe them as 'System', instead of 'Software') tools are designed to offer unequalled flexibility in combining and reconciling the work of multiple users. The analyst can selectively consolidate and separate, either whole, or partial encyclopaedias, or selected objects and maintain multiple encyclopaedias for different projects or users.

For an IT department to be a valued contributor to the company's success, its staff must be supplied with tools to respond effectively to business opportunities, where CASE tools can assist in the full life cycle of the applications development.

Applications which reduce costs, add value, and show effectiveness. For IT to be a valued contributor in business, its functions, and service to users must be highly adaptive, in planning, manufacturing, products design, marketing, and the overall company culture. To succeed in such concepts, IT conducts an inter-departmental analysis of its information systems, to assess its assets and capabilities.

As part of the new concepts, IT will bring forward a long range strategic plan for business systems. Evolve from a business system planning to an overall technical architecture planning approach. Tools, including CASE, are the key to the success of the overall technical architecture.

From the user perspective, the analysis of problems is critical. Detailed analyses of the operating systems, the manual systems, and the functional relationships will serve the purpose of the overall architecture. A CASE tool is highly instrumental, in being able to present the numerous applications to management and users and to gain consensus among the staff.

One of the strengths of the CASE tool is its ability to hold information, definitions, and comments. With a user-friendly tool, the analyst finds it easier to start and modify the diagrams. The users understand what the IT is doing. Pictures generated out of the tool are shown to the users for consensus and where necessary the diagrams get back into the tool to redraw.

The tool makes it easy. Diagrams are redrawn quickly and using the tool causes the analysts and users to question the analysis more. The result is a better quality system.

The CASE tool will prompt the analyst to begin with a decomposition of the areas that are involved and then a global data model which can be used as the starting point for the data model side of the project. These are explained to the users. In doing so, the design tool makes things easier. The analyst can move things around on the screen, which encourages modular design techniques.

As explained, the IT project team is responsible for the research and development of the advanced concepts and technologies in support of the company's information systems. The IT department is not only responsible for the traditional data administration duties, but also for the introduction of the CASE tools and the building up of the encyclopaedia.

CASE tools are a fairly new technology and systems engineers are still finding many ways to implement the potentials offered. Some CASE tools are design to be modular with separate tools for planning, analysis, and design and application generation. These tools can work together as a single integrated product, or separately as individual ones.

At the end of the day, no matter what anyone may say, a CASE tool, or any product may fail the IT department and the business as a whole, unless a properly documented system requirements specification is produced. A specification upon which everything will depend - to deliver what the user asked.

By now, all the phases, starting from the Project Initiation Document (PID), right through to the required analysis, the users' problems and requirements cataloguing, their solutions and the specification of the required system, all are complete. The next step is for the users to sign off this phase of the module, prior to starting on the building of the system.

The reader will appreciate that the volume of the documentation of the complete study of this fictional module may consist of more than one thousand pages. In view of this, only a few examples are selected as extracts of the system requirement specification. The full documentation of a module such as the example presented usually takes a small team of people a few months to complete.

Therefore, only one example of each one of the following is included in this book:

- Functional Decomposition Diagram and Report,
- Data Model Subset Diagram and Components,
- Data Inventory,
- Dataflow Diagrams Set and Descriptions,
- Functions,
- Transactions,
- Events,
- Problems and Requirements Catalogue,
- Solutions,
- Menu and Screens Reports.

Once all above are inserted in the CASE tool, the automatic outputs, included in the specifications, individually show the listing of all the components, within each picture, with the appropriate descriptions for each component. Every one of the components is associated to each other.

INFORMATION SYSTEMS EXPLAINED

It is hard to imagine business today without information systems. Information Technology in general is an important part of business and everyday life. It has become very important for individuals and organisations, in the ability to compete, perform and prosper.

As a support structure and as a tool for business, systems can deliver a number of significant benefits. Costs can be reduced, productivity increased, services improved and profits enhanced.

People at the sharp end of business want a better understanding of the way that systems are developed and function. It is hoped that in this book systems issues are explained and that the I.T. logical analysis helps people to comprehend the broad aspects of technologies available to assist in achieving personal and business objectives.

Systems ought to be about enabling business and personal change.

COMMERCE AND THE INTERNET

The term 'Electronic Commerce' (e-commerce) is commonly used to mean doing business electronically. It is the paperless exchange of critical business information between companies and their suppliers, government departments, financial institutions, customers and companies, even within organisations.

Business today sees the electronic commerce as a way to streamline operations, reach new markets, and serve their clients more efficiently. It can often be a catalyst for business change through business process re-engineering. A streamlined new process nearly always entails some degree of automation. Since many business processes cut across boundaries between departments, divisions and even companies, electronic commerce is a natural way to automate these processes.

A popular method of communication for exchanging data is Electronic Data Interchange (EDI). EDI may be defined as the 'exchange of standardised structured information between computer systems'.

EDI lends itself to the exchange of high volumes of information in a fixed format agreed by industry groups. This includes invoicing and payments, retail point-of-sale, bank transactions and manufacturing inventories. Because information is created and transferred electronically, there is no need for paperwork. This eliminated the need for re-keying data, which saves labour, speeds up processes and reduces details errors. Significant cost savings and reduced lead times can be achieved.

Processes can be automated and re-structured so that maximum operational efficiency is obtained. EDI operates by direct connection between users and over private and public data networks, ensuring privacy and security. As it uses highly structured formats, transmission speeds can be increased and overall costs reduced.

An e-commerce business solution relies on a network to act as a conduit for the transfer of data. Often, a 'value-added network' from a commercial provider is used, to provide the infrastructure required to transfer data securely and reliably among trading partners.

INTERNET IN BUSINESS

Until a few years ago, the Internet was not well known. One could scarcely have predicted the impact it would have on the world of systems and computers communications.

From its inception in the 1960s, the Internet evolved into a global network of business, academic and government computers. In recent years, businesses and individual users have recognised its potential as a way of communicating; by exchanging electronic mail, transferring files, accessing information services and communicating via bulletin boards, computer conferencing, and social interfacing.

The communication has been accompanied by the emergence of a part of the Internet known as the World Wide Web (WWW), which allows information to be presented in a graphical format; incorporating text, images, video and sound.

Any user with a suitable facility such as the latest mobile telephone, laptops, notebooks, personal computer (PC) can access the Web through a connection to the Internet using the wi-fi facility, broadband and the normal telephone land line.

Businesses are now setting up electronic shop-fronts and information sites on the Web and starting to realise the immense potential for reaching a global audience.

However, this open access to the vast storehouse of information raises a number of issues. The openness of the Internet leads to concerns over security. The Internet is a public set of networks that interconnect and are not inherently secure. As a consequence, there is a demand for effective software security tools known as 'firewalls'. These act as a secure gateway to limit outsiders' access to a company's data systems and provide control over staff access to the Internet.

Companies and individuals are reluctant to transmit and exchange sensitive details over the Internet, such as credit card information. The problem is now being addressed by developing effective encryption tools. The combination of firewalls and encryption will enable the realisation of the Internet's full commercial potential.

One genuine limiting factor on Internet usage is data transmission speeds. Although these have improved in recent years, for most users they remain painfully slow. It takes a few minutes to download and read even a basic Web page. Transferring large data files is often impracticably slow. These and other management issues associated with security, training and implementation, should be taken into account when considering the Internet as part of a personal or business strategy.

END

BIBLIOGRAPHY:

A Sofroniou, The Management Of Commercial Computing, PsySys Limited, ISBN: 0 9527956 0 4.

A Sofroniou, Structured Management Techniques, Association For Psychological Counselling And Training, Training Material, 1984.

A Sofroniou, Structured Systems Methodologies, Published and unpublished lecture notes, 1987 -1997.

A Sofroniou, Management Styles lectures, 1982.

A Sofroniou, Thesis submission on Automotive Components and Materials Purchasing System for Engineering Qualifications, 1983.

A Sofroniou, Collaborative project on Knowledge-base, Expert Systems and Artificial Intelligence, with Imperial College, Logica plc and The Engineering Industry Training Board, 1985-1986.

A Sofroniou, Rapid Structured Methodology for Life Assurance Systems, 1990-1992.

A Sofroniou, Analysis and Design project on EPoS Retail and Logistic System, 1995.

A Sofroniou, Research project, a study on COTS (Commercial Off The Shelf) Packages, 1995.

A Sofroniou, Technical Design projects for Internet Integration, Security, Client/Servers, Data Warehousing and Databases, 1996-1997.

A Sofroniou, The Year 2000 Project and Planning Procedures for European Group of Companies, 1998.

Ian Graham, Object Oriented Methods, Addison Wesley, ISBN: 0 201 56521 8.

E Yourdon and L Constantine, Structured Design, Yourdon inc., 1975.

Chris Gane and Trish Sarson, Structured Systems Analysis: Tools and Techniques, Improved System Technologies, Inc., 1977.